Greg Quill

1989 Live Reviews by Lenny Stoute

Kamin & Howell Inc.
Downsview, Ontario

Canadian Cataloguing in Publication Data

Quill, Greg
   The Rolling Stones 25th anniversary tour

ISBN 0-921458-02-9

1. Rolling Stones. 2. Rock musicians—England—
Biography. I. Title.

ML421.R64Q54 1989   784.5'4'00922   C89-
095328-7

Photography by Philip Kamin & Associates Inc.
Book Design by Judy Sherman/Mi Design
Production Coordination by W M Enterprises

TABLE OF CONTENTS   PAGE

The BAD BOYS of BRITISH ROCK

In 1970 the Rolling Stones made an outrageous claim. During the tour a year earlier that had yielded the live *Get Yer Ya-Yas Out!* album, someone in the entourage had been given permission to introduce this post-psychedelic, odds-and-sods, vaguely rhythm 'n' blues but decidedly British pop ensemble as "the greatest rock 'n' roll band in the world."

It was there, for all time, in the grooves of *Ya-Yas*, and it was, to most music fans, a cheeky and irreverent boast, flippant and disrespectful to the true fathers of rock 'n' roll—the likes of Chuck Berry, Jerry Lee Lewis, Elvis Presley, Howlin' Wolf, Bo Diddley, Muddy Waters—from whose original tune, "Rolling Stone Blues," the Stones had rather boldly taken their name.

"Rock 'n' roll" was, in 1970, an archaic tag, anyway. The Stones, defiant and rebellious since their formation in 1962, had resisted being tagged almost with a vengeance. Their sudden willingness to stake out an identifiable piece of musical turf seemed out of character.

When Mick Jagger, Brian Jones and Keith Richard (who later would pluralize his name legally to Richards) started out, playing "tributes" to archaic or little-known Chicago bluesmen in London's Marquee Club, they were just fragments in the infant British blues-revival movement, bit players to mainstage heroes, albeit underexposed ones, like Alexis Korner and John Mayall.

It was, without argument, primitive electric blues that first excited all three founding members of the Rolling Stones. But in subsequent years they experimented so wholeheartedly with other pop forms, with pseudo-classical and folk hybrids, with Eastern modes, British "beat" music and raw rhythm 'n' blues, and had prevailed as one of the hippest, most adventurous bands on the planet, that calling themselves "the greatest rock 'n' roll band in the world" seemed almost like a cheap and desperate grasp at a crown to which they had never been—nor even wanted to be—entitled.

That they almost immediately thereafter began redefining rock 'n' roll for the post-Woodstock generation was perhaps their greatest accomplishment. This was no idle boast, then; it was fact. For all time, rock 'n' roll bands will be measured against the Rolling Stones.

Theirs was an unlikely beginning. Streetwise suburban London schoolboys, Jagger and Richards first met at Dartford Maypole County Primary School. They were seven years old.

Ten years later, their mutual love of blues and American "rhythm music"—exotic tastes in Britain in those days—brought them together again. Richards had teamed up with guitarist Dick Taylor, a school chum at Sidcup Art School, and Jagger, studying at the London School of Economics, was jamming halfheartedly with

Taylor's band, Little Boy Blue and the Blue Boys.
Richards soon joined as second guitarist.

Their musical careers might have faltered then
and there. Jagger had a flair for business and the
instincts of a canny salesman. He was unusually
bright and self-confident, something of a social
climber, who at the same time was quite prepared
to shock polite company when it bored or angered
him. Unlike Richards, who took to performing
with a grudge but had something of the
perfectionist in him, Jagger "took the piss out of"
pop's base pretensions. His earliest performances
are remembered for his irreverent sexual swagger
and pout. He seemed to be satirizing the
exaggerated machismo of the very artists to
whom he said he was paying his respects.

Soon, those very gestures became his
trademark—appealing to his teenage fans,
horrifying to their mothers!

Not far away, at the Ealing Blues Club in
London, Richards, the more devoted blues
student, had begun sitting in occasionally with
an on-again-off-again aggregation known as Blues
Inc., whose new regular guitarist was a shaggy-
haired blond youth by the quite incredible name
of Elmo Lewis.

Lewis was, of course, an invention, one of a
dozen personas London-born Brian Jones had
assumed by the time he reached the age of 20.

By 1962, Jones was something of a local hero, a
notorious rebel with the heart and conscience of a
pirate. Born in reasonable affluence in
Cheltenham, he was rudderless, a drifter, even in
his pre-adolescent years. He was a gifted student
with "a profound artistic calling," according to
school reports, but apparently troubled and
undisciplined.

At the age of 16, Jones had forsaken his local
school to study jazz clarinet and saxophone with
local "be-bop" devotees, and had fathered two
illegitimate children. Attempting to avoid the
consequences, he fled briefly to Denmark and
Sweden, then returned to Cheltenham—and to
his latter girlfriend and child—as a reasonably
accomplished guitarist.

His ad-hoc family in tow, Jones was
drawn to London after a brief stint with a
local band, the Ramrods, and into the
burgeoning, post-Bohemian blues community,
where singer/harmonica player Alexis Korner
was king.

Within weeks, Jones—as Elmo Lewis—had
passed through Korner's domain and had all but
dug a niche for himself in London's new musical
culture as the leader of Korner's "B-grade"
incarnation of Blues Inc., which included Taylor,

pianist Ian Stewart and drummer and big-band jazz devotee Charlie Watts.

Encouraged by Jones, Richards and Jagger became increasingly popular "off-night" guests of, then featured performers with, Blues Inc.

And almost overnight, the Rolling Stones were born.

Jones, Jagger and Richards, inspired only by the long-distance echoes of Chicago bluesmen they obtained in out-of-the-way import-record stores, had formed a pact of sorts. In fact, they'd begun sharing a bedsitter in the middle of London and spent their meager earnings on a demo tape. Featuring Stewart, Taylor on bass and Tony Chapman on drums, it was rejected by EMI, the company that would, a few months later, sign the Beatles.

Stewart's salary as an underling in a London chemical company paid for rent and food. But that wasn't enough for Dick Taylor, who bailed out of the band—only to return for the Rolling Stones' first official performance July 12, 1962, at the Marquee as a "one-off favor" to his musical colleagues.

The first Rolling Stones comprised Jagger, Jones, Richards, Taylor and drummer Mick Avory, a ringer for the night who'd later be a founding member of the Kinks. He was replaced almost immediately by Tony Chapman, and Taylor's slot was filled by journeyman bassist Bill Wyman, a member of a blues-and-rockabilly outfit known as the Cliftons, and seven or eight years older than his new partners. He was not expected to take the pace the others had set.

► *Bill Wyman in the height of fashion for 1969.*

Chapman was something of a misfit, too, and after an auspicious debut, the Rolling Stones remained a nonperforming entity for some months until they persuaded Watts, who'd left Blues Inc. for a safe job with an advertising company, to give up the good life for . . . who knew what?

Watts joined in January, 1963, on the promise of a residency at London's Crawdaddy Club, a hip blues joint run by Giorgio Gomelsky, who was attracted by the odd, unstable chemistry of the Stones and gambled on the band's appeal. The gamble paid off; the band was a nonstop hit at Crawdaddy for eight or nine months, a run that had been equaled by only one other band—although in the inconsequential northern port city of Liverpool, and in a dank cellar called the Cavern.

By the end of 1962, the Beatles had emerged as the heroes of British pop. They'd learned the basics of America's new musical culture very quickly, had reinterpreted them and were riding the crest of a national wave of admiration that would soon roll across the Atlantic.

By then, too, the Beatles were being managed by Brian Epstein, the record retail executive who'd cleaned up their image, styled their hair, tailored their suits and encouraged their naturally witty, wise-cracking repartee with the press.

The Stones, now under the wing of Andrew Loog Oldham, their first full-time manager, would be something quite different—a raging, unkempt sort of Jerry Lee Lewis, say, to the Beatles' 1960s' version of Buddy Holly. Not that Loog Oldham had much of an argument from the band; in short order the new manager nudged out Stewart, a mild respectful lad who willingly became a road worker and occasional session pianist for the Stones, and re-made these rather upwardly mobile, upper-working-class lads into the nasties of British rock, the Beatles' foil, their sinister doppelganger.

"I never really liked the Beatles," Julia Lennon, John's sister, told me once. "I preferred the Stones; they were much more rebellious."

So it was, for almost the remainder of the decade—and perhaps for all time—that the Stones became the archetypal bad boys of British rock. British values are important here. The British as a nation, though in awe of American cultural traditions, were never fully respectful of them, except insofar as they could be adapted, reinterpreted. The British working class in particular, since before the French Revolution,

Keith and Mick grin at the irony of it all as rock's bad boys are inducted into the Hall Of Fame.

▲

Keith strains to hear a reporter's question during the tumultuous press conference announcing the Steel Wheels tour, in Grand Central Station.

were outspoken social critics, iconoclasts and political rebels.

To their own astonishment, the Beatles' frankness—on any issue—had a revolutionary impact in North America. If the Stones' music was more vulgar, more lascivious, Loog Oldham figured, what would America think of bad British boys who actually carried through Elvis's threat to ignite cultural, social and generational chaos?

It was an inspirational plan that would not be attempted again for more than a decade, when Malcolm McLaren unleashed the Sex Pistols in the late 1970s on a complacent, unprepared America.

The first step was to get a record out, something that would establish the new band's allegiance to black American music and distance them immediately from the Beatles, whose

heroes were largely white American rock and pop stars.

Trouble was, Lennon and McCartney had easily proven their worth as songwriters; no one in the Stones had actually got around to putting an original song together.

Not that it mattered. This was still an age in which performers rarely wrote; rather, they interpreted the work of professional songwriters, who rarely performed. The Beatles were something of an aberration in 1963.

In June that year, the Rolling Stones released their first single—Chuck Berry's "Come On"— and landed a couple of spots on national BBC TV pop shows, one at the first British national Jazz and Blues Festival in Richmond. Late in the year they were part of a touring package that included the Everly Brothers, Bo Diddley and Little

Richard. After a Stones' performance on *Thank Your Lucky Stars,* a TV show, Loog Oldham was told by the show's producer to "chuck that vile-looking singer with the tire-tread lips," advice at which the hip young businessman only snarled.

Things were on the move. "Come On" made it to the British top 30, and the Stones' second single, Lennon and McCartney's "I Wanna Be Your Man," cracked the top 15.

Then, third time lucky, the Rolling Stones, coming off their first headlining tour of Britain—with the Ronettes, of all people—broke the top 5 in January, 1964, with a wild and near-chaotic version of Buddy Holly's Bo Diddley-inspired "Not Fade Away."

That was the single that introduced the band to Americans, who bought the record in sufficient numbers to drive it halfway up the U.S. top 100.

Americans were well aware now of the powerful music young Britons were making. Grounded in black and rural American culture, this new pop was at once familiar and dangerous, "race music" reinvented for white kids. It was safe, yet not as safe nor as bloodless as the American radio pop—by the likes of Fabian and Pat Boone and Frankie Avalon—that had immediately preceded it. Besides, these were foreigners; they were exotic.

American teenagers were also well aware of the hysteria to which British youngsters were driven at the mere sight of the Beatles, and, in 1964, of the Stones. Already, though, lines were being drawn. The Stones were characterized by the British press—no doubt manipulated to a degree by Loog Oldham—as louts and hooligans. In photographs they looked sullen, unkempt, dirty. Cigarettes hung from their lips. They snarled in interviews, swore and, according to one sensationalistic story, thought nothing of urinating in public.

The music they made had no pleasing tone, no texture, no harmony, no symmetry. It was raw, abrasive, often out of tune, as if no thought had gone into it. These were slovenly street kids with a grudge against society, and their performances were orgiastic rituals without form or meaning.

What the Beatles did with sheer craftsmanship, the Rolling Stones achieved by allowing themselves to be seen as possessed by the spirit of rock 'n' roll. Their obsession with "the beat," with the raw, elemental demands of rock music, was manifested physically in Jagger's grotesque facial expressions and uncoordinated gestures, in Richards's thick, crackling chords, in Jones's sudden flights of electric fantasy.

Rolling Stones' Manager Andrew Oldham (L) with Charlie Watts and Bill Wyman on British TV series 'Ready.Steady.Go'
▼

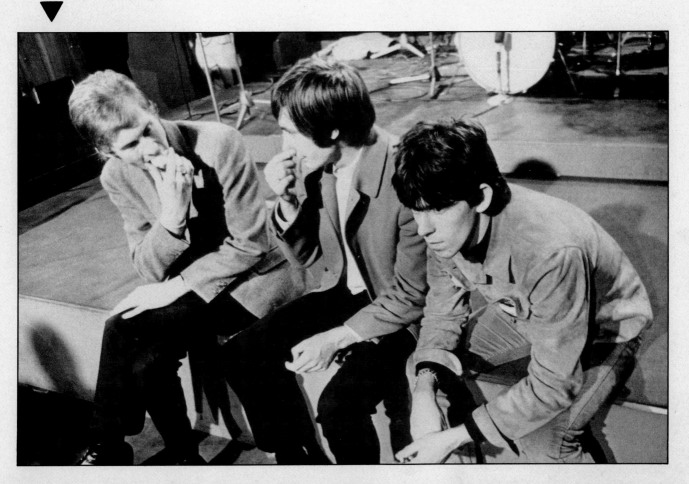

▶ *The Rolling Stones' first T.V. appearance, for the British pop music series 'Ready. Steady. Go', 1963.*

You had to be a rebel to get off on the Stones. A suspect in society, a misfit.

Within two months of the release of their first album—*The Rolling Stones*—in April, 1964, the band was on tour in the United States. Buoyed by the enormous success of "It's All over Now," a driving rhythm 'n' blues classic by Bobby Womack, which had already been a moderate hit in America for the Valentinos and was now the Stones' first number-one British single, the band caused a sensation.

In Chicago, where they recorded the 5 × 5 EP, a scheduled press conference was aborted when fans started rioting. The hysteria only became fiercer after American radio stations banned the Stones' next single, the blues standard "Little Red Rooster," because its lyrics were interpreted as sexually explicit.

By late 1964 Jagger and Richards, inspired by the staggering publishing and songwriting royalties Lennon and McCartney were accruing, formed a tentative composing partnership, initially under the pseudonym Nanker Phelge. If the gatekeepers of American morality had found old blues lyrics objectionable, they'd have slammed the doors then and there on the Rolling Stones if they'd known what revenge Jagger and Richards were about to exact. After the Glimmer Twins, as the writing duo was soon to be known, found their voice, rock 'n' roll lost its innocence forever.

RUDE, LEWD...
and BEAUTIFUL

The year 1965 was a watershed year for the Stones. In January, "The Last Time," a Jagger-Richards song, hit the number-one spot in Britain and landed in the American top 10, followed by "Satisfaction," which made the number-one position all over the world. "Tell Me," "Time Is on My Side" and "Get off My Cloud," each an original composition, were all top-20 hits by midyear.

That year the band's accumulated LP output in the world market included *12 x 5, The Rolling Stones Now!, Out of Their Heads* and *December's Children (and Everybody's).* Critics in the years since have noted that the band's earliest work still rates as some of the hardest rhythm 'n' blues and neo-Chicago blues ever recorded by a white band.

The band's fascination with urban black music continued through *12 x 5,* which included a durable revision of "Under the Boardwalk," but also marked a turning point. The Stones were no longer content to be blues revisionists; they wanted now to make their own music. *Aftermath,* their first album of all-original songs, was overshadowed in 1966 by the Beatles' *Revolver* and Bob Dylan's finest album, *Blonde on Blonde.* It was a year of marvelous musical accomplishments, probably unequaled in pop history, Yet, against the stream, the Stones managed to make their mark with "Ruby Tuesday," a pseudo-Elizabethan ballad, and "Paint It Black," a somber evocation of nihilism induced by lost love, rendered in almost Eastern chromatic modes. Both made it to the top of the American charts in 1966, a year after the band made its debut on U.S. TV on the influential Ed Sullivan Show, and in 1967.

In the same period they released the *Got Live If You Want It* LP and scored a handful of other top-10, -20 and -30 hits in Europe, Australia, Britain and the U.S.—"Mother's Little Helper," 19th Nervous Breakdown," "Have You Seen Your Mother, Baby (Standing in the Shadows)?" and "Lady Jane," another ornate ballad that proved again how thoroughly Richards and Jagger were learning the basics of serious composition.

It was not, however, the mastery of lyrical songwriting for which the Stones were loved—and loathed—in America. Eschewing the tailored wholesomeness of the Beatles for a threatening, rebellious stance had almost become a way of life for the band. In fact, in a strange way, Brian Epstein managed the Stones' fate as well as that of his mop-topped charges; Jagger and his self-styled Cockney street louts only had to react to—or against—whatever their more successful colleagues did. All part of a deliberated, well-conceived career plan.

And remembering how Elvis had once used TV to staggering effect, by forcing the medium's gatekeepers to censor his swiveling hips, the Stones created a sensation in January, 1967, with their performance on the Ed Sullivan show of

▲

Keith and Ron visit with r'n'b artist Don Covey while all concerned were recording in N.Y.

"Let's Spend the Night Together." It was not a song that endeared itself to America's parents. It confirmed the worst fears about their sons and daughters—that listening to rock 'n' roll was essentially an act of defiance against authority, and that rock music itself incited children to sexual sin.

In retrospect the performance was pretty tame. On air, Jagger actually mumbled the offensive line, which had been deleted, or replaced by "Let's spend some time together," on U.S. pressings of the single. Still, it was a daring, provocative gesture, one more in an accumulating series, and one for which the Stones would soon pay.

A month later Jagger and Richards were arrested and charged in London for possession of drugs, and in May, Brian Jones, too, fell afoul of Britain's tough anti-narcotics laws. In the increasingly hostile battle for social and cultural power, the charges won the Stones few friends and not much sympathy from the new political underground, though the heavy jail sentences imposed on the three men were eventually suspended after lengthy legal appeals.

Publicly chastised, the Stones kept a low profile for the next six months while Jagger and his girlfriend, singer Marianne Faithfull, joined the Beatles on vacation at the retreat of transcendentalist Maharishi Mahesh Yogi in India, while Jones and Richards started work on the album that would become *Their Satanic Majesties Request*—a quite deferential response to the Beatles' psychedelic masterpiece, *Sergeant Pepper's Lonely Hearts Club Band*.

By early 1968 the Stones had scored another couple of hits—"We Love You," with Lennon and McCartney singing backup, "Dandelion" and "She's a Rainbow"—and American lawyer Allen Klein, whom McCartney would later blame for hastening the dissolution of the Beatles, had replaced Loog Oldham as manager of the Rolling Stones.

In May, 1968, with the release of "Jumping Jack Flash," the band gave notice that it was possessed of a new vision, a sinewy strength all its own. A catharsis had taken place, one not fully realized until the *Beggar's Banquet* LP finally, five months later, disentangled itself from the cluster of record-company objections over apparently distasteful cover photographs.

It was the Stones' finest, bravest achievement, a witty and adventurous album colored by Jones's remarkably clever arrangements and new musical textures—marimba, sitar, dulcimer,

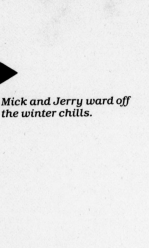

Mick and Jerry ward off
the winter chills.

mandolin, Latin percussion. *Washington Post* critic Carl Bernstein called *Beggar's Banquet* the band's "rawest, lewdest, most arrogant, most savage record yet," adding, "and it's beautiful!"

It contained several masterpieces, landmark performances, including the anarchic rant "Street Fighting Man," Jagger's meanest misogynist tract, "Stray Cat Blues," and "Sympathy for the Devil," a brilliantly condensed and bitterly skewed essay on the forces propelling civilization. French movie director Jean-Luc Godard used actual session footage of the "Sympathy" recording in his first English-language effort, *One Plus One*, which was later expanded—without Godard's approval—to include more images of the Stones, and retitled after the band's apocalyptic rock epic.

GIMME SHELTER

As successful as *Beggar's Banquet* was, the Stones continued to be plagued by personnel, image and legal problems. On June 9, 1969, Jones, the band's most astute and curious musician, let it be known that he wanted out of the Rolling Stones by announcing, "I no longer see eye-to-eye with the others over the discs we are cutting."

Closer to the truth, Jones had developed a serious drug habit and had simply lost the will and the physical strength to continue. He was less at odds with the band over music—*Beggar's Banquet* had been widely hailed as Jones's singular triumph—than he was out of touch spiritually and mentally with his colleagues.

He was replaced the following week by guitarist Mick Taylor, a John Mayall's Bluesbreakers alumnus and a thoughtful, intelligent, if unadventurous player. And on July 3, long before he could begin putting his own band together, as he'd promised fans, Jones was found dead in his swimming pool. Citing the cause of death as "misadventure," the London coroner closed the lid on rumors of suicide, accidental overdose and murder. Whatever tortured Brian Jones in his final months will never be fully known, except perhaps by the remaining Stones.

Two days after his death, the band staged a free memorial concert at Hyde Park, where Jagger read excerpts from the Romantic poet Shelley and set free 3,500 butterflies in tribute to Jones. On July 11, one day after their former colleague's funeral, the Stones released the single that was to enshrine them in the pop pantheon as new-age rock 'n' roll revisionists. "Honky Tonk Women," a stunning and powerful amalgam of Southern roadhouse blues and primping male sexuality, laid the foundation for the subsequent claim that the Stones, by now, were the world's best rock 'n' roll band.

That reputation was enhanced time and again during the 1969 tour of America. Delayed while Jagger completed work in Australia on the poorly received Tony Richardson movie *Ned Kelly*, the tour was memorable for the attendance records it broke and for Jagger's overwhelming performances. Highlights of the 1969 show, which showcased material for the *Let It Bleed* album—a sardonic, thumbs-up response to the Beatles' sentimental "Let It Be," featuring guitar tracks both by Jones and Taylor—included a near chaotic "Gimme Shelter" and a 15-minute version of "Midnight Rambler," in which Jagger seemed to relish in an act of stylized rape by whipping the air with his belt and using the microphone as a less-than-allegorical symbol of phallic power.

The hysteria, fueled by the Stones' apparent affection for the dark Satanic side of human nature, grew white hot during those weeks in America and exploded disastrously at the final concert, billed as a free gesture of gratitude to

▲

Mick displays his most valuable assets.

U.S. fans, at Altamont Speedway in California on December 6.

Poorly organized and ill-conceived, the event was overshadowed by cold weather, black clouds and an ominous sense of foreboding, which intensified when it was learned that the Stones—allegedly on the advice of San Francisco's Grateful Dead—had hired, for $500 worth of beer, the local chapter of the Hell's Angels motorcycle gang to be the site security force.

Already saddled with a reputation for inciting violence among fans in America, the Stones bore the full brunt of public outrage when the Angels rode roughshod through the crowd, beating concert-goers with lead-trimmed pool cues and stabbing one young spectator to death in full view of the band.

The performance, the abuse, the murder, and finally, Jagger's denial of responsibility for the tragedy, were captured in *Gimme Shelter,* a grim documentary movie by the Maysles brothers. It was one of the most potent indictments of rock 'n' roll savagery ever made.

Under increasing media pressure and genuinely frightened by their misdirected power, the Stones dropped "Sympathy for the Devil" from their stage shows until 1975.

For the following 18 months, the band steered clear of America, concentrating instead on less excitable British and European audiences. The live *Get Yer Ya-Yas Out!,* a memento of the American tour, was released in mid-1970 and, like *Let It Bleed,* went gold ($1 million in sales) in short order. The following year saw the formation of the Stones' own label, distributed by Atlantic Records, with the lascivious tongue-and-lips logo—designed by New York's prominent avant-garde pop-art guru, Andy Warhol—that graced the 1971 LP, *Sticky Fingers.* The album cover featured the Warhol-designed zippered and bulging male crotch shot, and contained the hits "Brown Sugar"—a swaggering sexual brag very much in the "Honky Tonk Women" vein—and "Wild Horses," which Jagger and Richards had written for California country-rockers the Flying Burrito Brothers, whose version had displeased the Glimmer Twins.

Other projects were undertaken during 1971. Jagger starred in *Performance*, British film-maker Nicholas Roeg's paean to moral decadence, took part in recording the movie's soundtrack, which yielded the sinister "Memo to Turner," a minor hit, and married Bianca Perez Morena de Macias, a wealthy Nicaraguan socialite and fashion model.

Their glittering union and obvious appetite for the high life seemed to alienate Jagger from the other Stones and created suspicion among fans that he had sold out, lost his rock 'n' roll edge.

Those fears were put to rest when the band started work on *Exile on Main Street*, arguably one of the finest pieces in the entire rock 'n' roll repertory.

Exile, a double album released early in 1972, was a huge bowl of life-affirming passion for the purely physical. Mean, lean, cacaphonic, raw and elemental, it brought the Stones back into the vanguard with the hits "Tumbling Dice and Happy," and back into the American spotlight.

Mick and Andy Warhol autograph Andy's series of art prints of Mick.

▼

TWO STEPS
FORWARD
ONE STEP BACK

When the Stones returned to the United States in the summer of 1972, revitalized by the *Exile* sessions and by the critical acclaim heaped on the album, it was clear they'd lost nothing of their edge, nor the affection of their audiences.

In fact, the 1972 extravaganza, during which Jagger was hailed by critics as "the single most exciting musical performer at work at this moment" and "charismatic, dynamic, glorious, riveting," broke all the band's existing attendance records and hauled in a massive—for then—$3 million at the box office.

By now it was also clear that the Stones were grown men fueled no longer by rebellious arrogance, but by the heady rush of big business dealings. The bad boys of rock 'n' roll had become cross-media superstars, and during three subsequent sold-out tours of the U.S., spaced three years apart (1975, 1978 and 1981), lived in the rarefied atmosphere inhabited only by the very rich, the powerful and the very beautiful. Jagger and Bianca, with their daughter, Jade (born in October, 1971), were the darlings of international high society, and traveled to its various outposts in the world's most exotic cities, collecting art, clothes, antiques, property, wine and cars.

Again, however, the demands of the high life weakened the Stones' commitment to rock 'n' roll. Few fans and fewer critics were impressed by 1973's *Goat's Head Soup* album, generally acknowledged as the band's poorest effort, as unfocused as *Their Satanic Majesties Request*, but less genuinely adventurous, though it yielded two hits—"Angie" in 1973 and "Heartbreaker" the following year.

That album, and its successor, *It's Only Rock 'n' Roll,* were perhaps the lowest musical points in the Stones' career. Dismissed by critics as "mere product," as "craft in an unheroic form," as passable boogie without inspiration, neither record advanced the band's boast that it was the best in the world. The hits on *It's Only Rock 'n' Roll*—"Starfucker (Star Star)," a remake of the Temptations' "Ain't Too Proud to Beg" and "If You Don't Rock Me"—certainly sounded like the Stones, but like the Stones of three or four years earlier. These were depressingly stagnant records, retrograde performances, annoyingly devoid of power and imagination.

And from 1972 the band's stage show began to show signs of, if not fatigue, then certainly boredom and cynicism.

That first U.S. tour with Taylor was, perhaps necessarily, marked by a sense of contrition. Jagger was no longer a demonic presence, but something of a buffoon, a village idiot controlled by a larger mechanism. Wyman and Watts, never known for their dynamism, seemed more withdrawn and self-conscious than ever. And Taylor, delicately handsome and vulnerable, was a friendly, if unspectacular contributor to the mix, a graceful waffler rather than a didactic musician, like Richards, the only Stone who never seems to have lost his anger and energy. If the 1972 tour is remembered as the one in which the Stones exulted in the pure professionalism of their own style of rock 'n' roll, it's because Richards's dirty, dangerous guitar work and stage antics undercut the sheer gloss and size of this new industrial-strength juggernaut.

For reasons that have never been fully disclosed, Taylor quit the Stones after *It's Only Rock 'n' Roll*. Musicians close to him balanced his decision to forego inevitable wealth and superstardom as a member of the world's best-known rock outfit with his distaste for the rock 'n' roll life-style and with his conviction that this particular band was not making, or even attempting to make, proper use of his talents.

That Taylor was subsequently never able to make a musical mark as significant as those he made with the Stones is the price he paid for quitting.

The band, of course, rolled right on, burying the memory of Taylor—as they'd buried the memory of Jones before him—with a stunning new album, *Made in the Shade*, which introduced a potential replacement, guitarist Ron Wood.

Apparently willing to share Wood, a long-time friend of both Richards and Jagger, with Rod Stewart and the Faces, whose guitar position he had held for years, the Stones made a raw, broadly stroked, rapidly recorded album that bristled with defiance.

The subsequent tour, with Wood in place on stage, revealed a tougher, more athletic and harder-working band. Jagger this time resembled

◄

Mick, the casual aristocrat.

Mick during the 1982 European Tour, Frankfort, Germany.

nothing so much as an obsessed aerobics coach, reveling in the sheer physical stress of performance, rather than in the magic of rock 'n' roll itself. Wood, a slightly younger and healthier version of the dissipated Richards, formed a gritty, sneering two-man cabal with his mentor, and did much to restore a certain appealing brutality to the Stones' music.

Still, it wasn't until 1976 and the *Black and Blue* album that the band made its first perceivable musical steps forward in many years. With the problem of a permanent replacement for Taylor yet unresolved, *Black and Blue* featured a host of session players, every one of them rumored to be in line for the job.

Having unsuccessfully wooed American blues guitarist, the late Roy Buchanan, and slide player Ry Cooder—both contenders even before Taylor's appointment—the Stones finally made Wood an offer he could not refuse. The Faces folded within weeks.

Black and Blue met with ambiguous reviews. Some critics, appalled by the controversial publicity campaign featuring shots of a partially bound, semi-naked and clearly battered woman, found nothing redeeming in the music, which seemed, in "Fool to Cry" and "Hot Stuff," to make a reluctant and cheap concession to disco music, generally reviled by serious rock fans.

Yet the album was an energetic departure from well-worn territory, a celebratory return to the Stones' rhythm 'n' blues roots, and it put the two previous efforts well into the shadows. It also gave warning that the bad boys were back. Worse, these were full-grown rock 'n' roll outlaws now, with serious and sophisticated habits and obsessions. Jagger's sojourn among the jet-set was over, his marriage well and truly on the rocks, and he was eager, in the heady, glittering and superficial late-1970s, for a taste of the street again.

Richards, on the other hand, had sublimated his passion for the real world—along with most other passions—with heroin and cocaine, and was arrested and charged in Toronto in February, 1977. He faced deportation—and denial of all future visa applications—from Canada if convicted of possession and trafficking.

His longtime girlfriend, Anita Pallenberg, had been arrested for marijuana possession at Toronto's international airport the day before the Royal Canadian Mounted Police raided the guitarist's downtown hotel room on a warrant substantiated by the charges against Pallenberg.

▶

The twins of twang harmonize.

It had been the Stones' intention to record an album in Canada, but after the bust and the subsequent sentence—Richards was ordered to perform a fund-raising charity concert for the Canadian National Institute for the Blind within 12 months—those plans were abandoned in favor of a grand public-relations gesture, the brainchild of the band's new manager, former British secret-service intelligence agent Peter Grant, who also directed the careers of Southern rockers Lynyrd Skynyrd and Australian country-rock band, the Dingoes.

The gesture, disguised as a recording session for a possible future live album, was an all-night performance in Toronto's then premier rock-concert club, El Mocambo, capacity 300. Supposedly a secret, the show attracted thousands of fans, who stood outside the club for hours hoping for a glimpse of, or the sound of a few distant chords from, their heroes.

Inside, the performance—as well as the invited celebrities—created a sensation. It was, after all, the Stones' first club date since 1964, the first time the band had been on such intimate terms with an audience in more than 13 years.

The audience, which included Montreal band April Wine, the show openers, was a cross section of Canadian and American rock-industry movers and shakers, but it had a star of its own—Margaret Trudeau, the young and soon-to-be-estranged wife of Canadian Prime Minister Pierre Trudeau. Inflaming sensation into spectacle, Mrs. Trudeau had arrived at the club with Jagger in his limousine, apparently as his date, and apparently unfazed at accompanying the associate of a man who was at that very time on

continued on page 65

Ron Wood has blended into the Stones as if he's always been one. ◀

The Stones announce the Steel Wheels Tour from Grand Central Station, N.Y. ▼

EXTRA

★ THE DAILY TRIBUNE ★

POPE DECLARES:
KEITH RICHARDS IS GOD

With a growing family to support, Keith Richards moonlights as a paperboy.

**Mick goes shirtless in
public for the last time,
Sept. 1981.**

**The uplifting finale for the
shows on the 1981 tour.** ▼

Jagger storms through
"Throw Away" at the
Country Club, October
1988.

At the Country Club in L.A.
Mick debuts his 1988
Touring Band, featuring
Jeff Beck.

▲ Keith Richards and Ron Wood
support Bob Dylan
at the Live Aid Benefit Concert,
July 13, 1985.

The Rolling Stones are
inducted into the Rock 'n'
Roll Hall of Fame. ▼

The quintessential Jagger snarl.

Bill and Mandy try to catch the waiter's eye.

Jagger visits with Pete Townsend on The Who's 1982 Tour.

Steve Jordan points out Keith to a confused photographer.

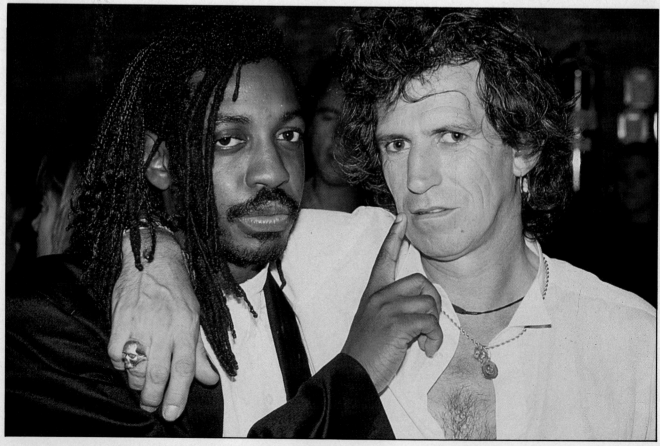

-EXCLUSIVE-

1989

TOUR

PHOTOS

▲ Ron and Keith trade
babysitting tips.

Mick leans into "Rock and
a Hard Place". Toronto,
Sept. 3, 1989. ▼

2,000 light years from
home.

"You're Not the Only
One . . ."

▶ " . . . With Mixed Emotions . . . "

▼ "You're Not the Only Ship, Adrift on the Ocean". MIXED EMOTIONS.

Mick tries to follow
Ronnie's lead.

The group in full jam on
"Tumbling Dice". ▼

Charlie Watts is arguably the most versatile drummer in rock.

▶
Absorbed in the Blues.

A rare shot of Bill Wyman moving.
▼

*"Don't play with me,
'cause you're playing
with fire."*

▲ *The boys wave good-bye to Toronto. Sept. 4, 1989.*

Keith's intensity surprises Ron. ▼

continued from page 32

bail and awaiting trial for one of the most serious offenses in the Canadian criminal code. Mrs. Trudeau, who maintained throughout that she was acting with her husband's and children's approval, was spotted in Jagger's company in other North American cities in the weeks following. Her activities sparked a public uproar that almost cost the federal Liberal government its leadership.

Months later, the Canadian courts were satisfied that Richards had kicked his drug habit, and he begged lenience. The performance he was ordered to give, by way of paying back society for his breaches, was eventually staged at a CNIB auditorium in Oshawa, a satellite city east of Toronto. It caused organizers and the institute itself a host of security and public-relations problems that exacted a heavier toll on them than the sentence did on Richards. He played in the suburban music hall with a pickup group, the New Barbarians, that included Ron Wood, jazz bassist Stanley Clarke and Ziggy Modeliste, drummer for a New Orleans rhythm 'n' blues band, the Meters.

Jagger rampages at Rich Stadium, Buffalo, 1981.

The SEEDS of
DISSOLUTION

Adversity becomes the Rolling Stones. In the past decade, despite considerable disagreement between Jagger and Richards over the appropriateness of men in their 40s continuing in the often trivial and necessarily juvenile pursuit of rock 'n' roll glory, the band has never really looked back.

Black and Blue was followed in 1978 by *Some Girls*, the Stones' best-selling album to date and perhaps among their strongest musical efforts. It yielded another disco-influenced hit, "Miss You," a wry, tongue-in-cheek swipe at the pretensions of the era's dance-record makers that had Jagger swanning through the lead vocal in an uncharacteristic, shaky, but undeniably appealing, falsetto. The LP also paid tribute, in "Shattered," to new, minimalist rock 'n' roll influences in the wake of the punk movement.

But again, the Stones free-and-easy and apparently offhand attempts to make light of sexual and ethnic stereotypes in the title track aroused the ire of feminists throughout the world. The bitter public protest culminated in injunctions by some of the women featured in the "mug shot" lineup in the cover art—the late Lucille Ball was among those who took particular offense—to prevent distribution of the album.

The band redeemed itself somewhat in 1980, with *Emotional Rescue,* lost faith again with fans in 1981 with the lackluster *Sucking in the Seventies*, a throwaway effort that included the live El Mocambo material. It may have suffered most from Jagger's disinterest with music and his fascination with lanky Texas model Jerry Hall, who would eventually bear him two children. But later that year, they scored again with the more conventional and definitely less-disturbing rocker, *Tattoo You,* which, on the strength of demand created by a new generation of adolescent fans, outsold all its predecessors. This was an album in which the Stones emphasized their maturity—with the soothing and soulful "Waiting on a Friend," for example, and by adapting to brilliant effect the instrumental fills and solos of a jazz legend—tenor saxophonist Sonny Rollins. Yet, with "Start Me Up," which measured up admirably against "Brown Sugar" and "Honky Tonk Women," the band proved it was still capable of sweaty barroom boogie, that it was still the best and hardest rock band in the world.

Still Life, an unrewarding live memento of the 1981 world tour—with an estimated $20 million box-office take, it was the biggest-grossing rock tour to date—was popular largely among diehard fans. And quite unexpectedly, feature-film director Hal Ashby's full-length concert movie shot during the American part of the tour fared poorly in cinemas.

By the summer of 1983, amid rumors—started by Jagger himself—that the Stones were on the verge of dissolution, the band, now under its own management, had walked its label from long-time distributors Atlantic Records to CBS, where it

▲

*Ron and Keith bookend
Mick at Rich Stadium,
Buffalo, 1981.*

was guaranteed a record-breaking $6 million apiece for its next four LPs. CBS would soon cut a more expensive deal with Michael Jackson, but the Stones, for a couple of years, had the honor of being the wealthiest recording outfit in music history.

The band didn't waste time giving CBS its money's worth. *Undercover,* released in November, 1983, was an unabashedly gruesome piece of work, an electric shocker clearly designed to grab headlines, infuriate purists, offend public morals—and sell by the boxcar-load. With such titles as "Tie You Up," "Pretty Beat Up," "Too Much Blood," along with cover images and videos (banned in Britain by the BBC) that made graphic allusions to torture and violent death, *Undercover* was not so much a rock 'n' roll album as a grim and gory midway ride through a nightmare.

Undercover, for all the good it did the Stones, was a cynical effort, a hucksterish response to Jagger's growing conviction that rock 'n' roll was "a spent force . . . as music and as an instrument for social change," he said in the summer of 1981, when it seemed the band was on its last legs.

"It's merely recycling itself and I'm not that good a musician to break out of it. I can't go on leaping around forever—it would be unseemly. I could change my act and do more than just titillate little girls, but (I can't change) the

voice . . . ."

Eighteen months later, during the sessions that would result in the *Dirty Work* album, relations between Jagger and the other band members were reportedly strained. It was felt that Jagger had held back from the *Undercover* sessions many of his best songs for his solo album, *She's the Boss,* released a few months before *Dirty Work.* Though it failed to excite critics and sold considerably less than expected, Jagger's album added credence to rumors that his days with the Stones were over. And it was with some reluctance, apparently, that he rejoined his colleagues in Los Angeles to begin *Dirty Work* prior to their being honored—for the first time, since the Stones had never won a Grammy—with a lifetime-achievement award from the National Academy of Recording Arts and Sciences.

This time, however, in the wake of the embarrassing failure of his own solo album, Jagger was accusing Richards of withholding superior material for the guitarist's proposed solo album.

"They are friendly, but not friends," insiders reported.

Other members of the band seemed to be drifting away, too, in pursuit of creative and

financial buffers against the possible dissolution of one of the longest and most profitable partnerships in rock 'n' roll. In 1985 Wyman took it on himself to produce and promote an album of rock and rockabilly classics that would raise money for the Action Research into Multiple Sclerosis foundation (ARMS). The LP, *Willie and the Poor Boys,* included performances by drummers Watts, Kenny Jones and Terry Williams, guitarists Andy Fairweather Low and Jimmy Page, and singers Chris Rea and Paul Jones.

Watts was revisiting his past by assembling and eventually touring with a large and ungainly 35-piece big band comprising veteran British traditional jazz players. Wood, who married longtime girlfriend Jo Howard in London in January, 1985, was busy at work on his second solo album and jamming with anyone who'd come up with the price of a light ale.

▶

The richest pout in Rock.

RECONCILIATION
and ROLLING ON

Something happened late in 1985 that seemed to clear the air and bring Jagger and Richards to their senses. Insiders believe it was the death of pianist Ian Stewart, the 47-year-old "sixth Rolling Stone" and one of the band's founding members. Stewart, who continued to work as a road manager for the Stones and to perform on many of the band's records after being phased out of the live show in the 1960s, died of a heart attack.

"Without him there would have been no Rolling Stones," Wyman said. "He will be absolutely irreplaceable as a person and as a member of the group."

Whatever the reason, by the end of the *Dirty Work* sessions, the two leading members of the band had reconciled.

Featuring an exultant remake of the ancient rhythm 'n' blues hit "Harlem Shuffle," the album was a remarkably vital and cooperative effort whose purpose, Wood said, was "to turn the kids of today on to what we consider our roots."

As for Jagger, now 42, working with the Stones again was "like going back to an old shoe."

Featuring an all-star lineup of special guests, including Jamaican singer/songwriter Jimmy Cliff, R&B star Bobby Womack, singers Tom Waits, Ivan Neville and Kirsty McColl and guitarist Jimmy Page, *Dirty Work* reached back beyond electric blues to acoustic blues and early New Orleans jazz, and Watts's work was outstanding, authoritative. The LP was hot and raw at times, overlaid with searing guitars, but it wasn't an album that aimed to please Stones fans, nor was it a casual romp through typical rock 'n' roll preoccupations. In "Back to Zero," a new-age update of the sentiments expressed in *Sympathy for the Devil*, Jagger despaired for the future of mankind, and in the somber and disturbing "Sleep Tonight," where Richards made his first real mark as a lead singer, there was more than a hint of concern for the quality of life.

In retrospect, perhaps *Dirty Work*'s greatest achievement was in liberating Richards from his constraining "number two" position. His contributions here were more honest and heartfelt, more confident than anything he'd done on earlier records. Bitter at times, aggressive and deliberately provocative, particularly in his demands on Jagger, Richards used *Dirty Work* to pave the way for his first solo album, *Talk Is Cheap,* released in 1988.

But for the two years preceding Richards's emergence as a star in his own right—perhaps the most threatening omen in the band's history—the future of the Stones remained very much in doubt. Richards himself seemed to be all that was holding the band together.

Tanned, healthy, habit-free—with the exception, of course, of his lasting affection for bourbon—he had found unusual contentment in the spring of 1986 in his marriage to former

The exuberant closer to the 1981 tour as thousands of balloons soar skyward.

model Patti Hansen, who had already borne him one child and was about to give birth to their second.

The root of the Stones' problems during that period, he admitted, was that he wanted to tour—with the Stones, the band he believed would never die—and Jagger didn't. The rift between the two old friends opened when Jagger used an inordinate amount of time and energy to complete *She's the Boss*, the very existence of which the band had always resented.

"He was off doing videos and he couldn't put his full time into (*Dirty Work*) or the necessary couple of months for the studio," Richards said in April, 1986.

"Mick won't tour. Maybe he thinks it's too much of an athletic event. But when you work with somebody as many years as we have, you know this kind of feuding goes on all the time in one form or another.

"We can ride this out."

Ride it out they did. Even after Jagger performed with David Bowie and Tina Turner on the cross-Atlantic Live Aid and Nelson Mandela birthday telecasts for some 700 million TV viewers, and after the release of his second solo album, *Primitive Cool*, in the fall of 1987, the Stones were no closer to dissolution than they'd been at any time in the previous three years.

Friends said that Jagger and Richards had made a pact: if *Primitive Cool* failed to generate enough interest to warrant a solo tour, the Stones would continue. Others say Jagger's attempts to assume an elder statesman posture with his solo work, to write and sing about mature, adult issues, simply weren't rewarding.

The singer *did* perform a series of concerts in Japan in 1988, breaking a 12-year ban on Stones' personnel entering that country following allegations of drug use in previous trips. But even then, while Jagger dismissed the satanic antics that had made him famous as trappings of "a very extended silly season," he hinted that his old band would reunite for another album "and possibly another tour" the following year.

In August, 1988, bound for solo performances in Australia, Jagger confirmed to reporters at a London airport that the Stones were indeed planning a record to celebrate their twenty-fifth anniversary.

Apparently that was news to Richards. The band hadn't toured since 1982, and the *Dirty Work* sessions had left a bitter taste in his mouth. "Right in the middle of making (*Talk is Cheap*), just as I was on a roll, I get a call from Mick and the boys, saying, 'We need a meeting to talk

about getting back together again,'" he remembered. "'Are you trying to screw me up?'" he asked. "But of course it's the Stones, right? So I put everything on hold for a week and went to London."

Mind you, he didn't let his old partner off the hook easily. Jagger had "a Peter Pan complex" and broke with the band to compete with younger musicians, Richards told *Rolling Stone* magazine in September, 1988.

"Now he wants to put the Stones back together—because there's nowhere else to go."

It can't be that simple, of course. None of the Stones actually needs to keep this juggernaut on the road, as many younger critics pointed out when it was announced in April this year that the band was recording again and would go on tour in the late summer and fall for an estimated $65 million net.

Amid a crush of 1960s and 70s superstars called back to the circuit this year—including the Who, former Beatle Ringo Starr and an all-star ensemble, the Doobie Brothers and Little Feat— the Stones' reunion tour, promoted by Canada's Concert Productions International and Labatt Breweries, who beat out offers from veteran American concert producer Bill Graham, was greeted by many with cynicism.

In the wake of the tour announcement, Richards's induction into the "Legend" hall of fame by the newly established International Rock Awards organizers in a live television music special from New York in June was seen as little more than a pre-event publicity stunt. But in the weeks leading up to the start of the tour—in Philadelphia on September 1—the Stones have been basking again in the warm glow of public adoration.

Seeing them together again at a press conference in New York's Grand Central Station, where the band played taped snippets from its new *Steel Wheels* album for a large assembly of astonished and admiring music journalists, no one doubted that the Rolling Stones are rock 'n' roll incarnate; that, with hearts on sleeves and ragged edges still flapping in a revolutionary breeze, these five men have continued to temper their spirit in the same flames they ignited in 1964. The Stones have never failed to deliver, never faltered, never refused a challenge, never weakened in their resolve to shake things up.

Steel Wheels, a sharp and brutal album that celebrates that continuing passion, that raw, savage affection for the most primal forms of musical communication, is proof that the Stones still roll. And for the same reasons—"love, fame and fortune," as Jagger said—as they always have.

The Stones accept the plaudits of Philadelphia, Aug. 31, 1989.

▼

STONES

BIOGRAPHIES

MICK JAGGER

*July 26, 1943. Michael Philip Jagger is born in Dartford, Kent, England. One of two sons of Eva and Joe Jagger, a physical-education instructor, then senior lecturer at Strawberry Hill, Britain's leading physical-training college, in Middlesex, Mick describes his childhood as "middle class" and "hard work." He enjoys history and sports, but despite his father's disapproval becomes obsessed, in his teenage years, with black American rhythm 'n' blues music. His brother, Chris, now takes care of Jagger's 20-bedroom country estate outside London.

*January, 1962. Jagger graduates from Dartford Grammar School and wins a government scholarship to study at the London School of Economics, which he attends through the end of 1964. In London he renews his friendship with former Dartford schoolmate, Keith Richards, and meets Brian Jones, a guitarist who shares their passion for electric blues. The three move into a delapidated Chelsea flat and make plans to form a band.

*July, 1962. Taking their name from Muddy Waters's "Rolling Stone Blues," Jagger, Jones, Richards, drummer Charlie Watts and bassist Bill Wyman make an impromptu debut at the Marquee, then a Soho jazz club, but win few friends with their long hair, sloppy clothes and Jagger's uncoordinated, uninhibited prancing.

*1967. After five top-selling albums and considerable success in Europe and the United States, Jagger, along with Jones and Richards, are convicted on relatively minor drug charges—Jagger is found guilty of possessing three pep pills, prescription items in Britain, but purchased legally in Italy—and sentenced to prison. After lengthy legal procedures and protest in the media against the stiffness of the sentences, Jagger's is eventually reduced by a higher court to a year's probation from three months in jail, and Richards's is overturned.

*1969. Jagger's first movie performance is in Nicholas Roeg's *Performance,* shot in 1968 and '69 and released in 1970. The singer plays a disillusioned, androgynous rock 'n' roller drawn into an obsessive relationship with a professional assassin, played by James Fox. In the same year, he plays the lead role in British director Tony Richardson's pallid movie biography of Ned Kelly, a late-nineteenth-century bushranger (outlaw) and Australia's most beloved folk hero. While filming in Australia, Jagger's girlfriend, Marianne Faithfull, almost dies in hospital after a self-administered heroin overdose. Some 20 years later, she says, "Going with Mick was a mistake. On the other hand, I learned a lot from him. As an education, it was invaluable. As a personal relationship, it was a disaster."

Jagger's image is not improved when it's learned it was his decision to hire Hell's Angels as the concert security force for the band's free

Brooke Shields and friends
chat up Keith backstage at
Philadelphia.

"thank-you America" show at the Altamont
Speedway near San Francisco in December,
1969. A young fan is stabbed to death by one of
the bikers while the Stones are performing.
*1971. Having dismissed marriage as "a pagan
rite," Jagger and Nicaraguan model and socialite
Bianca Perez Morena de Macias are wed on March
12 in St. Tropez, on the French Riviera. Bianca
gives birth to their daughter, Jade, in October
that year.

The marriage founders after about five years,
and Jagger vows he'll never attempt the vows
again.

"I'm almost Catholic in the way I feel about it,"
he says. "If you aren't successful at it, it isn't a
case of try, try again. I love women, I'm absorbed
by them. I have a lot of sympathy with women."
*1976. Japanese authorities ban the Rolling
Stones and the group's individual members from
the country after reports of past drug use. The
ban is lifted 12 years later, when Jagger
undertakes a record-breaking solo tour of Japan,
where 160,000 tickets to half a dozen venues sell
out in 60 minutes.
*March, 1977. Jagger is accompanied by
Margaret Trudeau, the young wife of Canadian
Prime Minister Pierre Trudeau, to Toronto's El
Mocambo, where the Stones perform their first
club show since 1964, and live tracks are
recorded for the *Sucking in the Seventies* album.

The Jagger-Trudeau alliance, following the arrest
of Keith Richards on charges for heroin
trafficking just days earlier, lasts for several
weeks, creating a public furor in Canada and
almost costing Trudeau his government.
*August, 1981. Jagger has an emerald, which
was set in his upper right incisor, replaced by a
small but expensive diamond, because friends
keep telling him he has a piece of spinach stuck
to his tooth.
*August, 1984. Elizabeth Scarlett, the first
daughter of Jagger and Texas model Jerry Hall, is
christened in London. Also in the British capital
at the time are Jade, the 13-year-old daughter of
the singer and Bianca Jagger, and Karis, also 13,
Jagger's "love child" from a relationship with
actress and singer Marsha Hunt. He pays more
than $2,000 a month for Karis's support and has
her sent as a boarder to the progressive Bedales
School in Hampshire, England, where Princess
Margaret's children were educated.

Jade, now 18, is working as a consultant and
editor on a documentary movie to celebrate the
Stones' twenty-fifth year as a rock 'n' roll band.

Jagger, described by his father as a caring parent "who doesn't spoil his children, (but) tries to make them aware of their own capabilities and gently stimulates them," and Hall have a second daughter in 1989. They have also "adopted" an Indian child under the Foster Parents Plan.

*October, 1986. Jagger releases *Running out of Luck*, an 80-minute video fantasy directed by Britain's Julien Temple and featuring nine songs from the singer's *She's the Boss* solo LP, released in 1985.

Of Hall, he says, "She's a nice, simple Texas girl and good fun. And she has her own job. Women should have jobs. Jerry makes money and that's one of the reasons
I like her."

*January, 1987. Hall is charged with possession of 20 pounds of marijuana in Bridgetown, Barbados. After a police investigation, charges are dropped.

*October, 1987. Jagger, 44, releases his second solo album, *Primitive Cool*, which he describes as "more reflective" than either his work with the Stones or his previous solo effort, *She's the Boss*, and as an album that deals with the preoccupations of a rock 'n' roll adult.

*April, 1988. Bronx reggae musician and composer Patrick Alley launches suit against Jagger for "stealing" the chorus section of "Just Another Night," Jagger's only hit from the *She's the Boss* LP, from Alley's own copyrighted song. After lengthy and often hilarious court hearings in which so-called experts from every level of the music industry testify the passages in question are both "virtually identical" and "totally dissimilar," and in which Jagger admits, "I don't really like that song," Alley's suit is dismissed.

*May, 1988. An Austrian novelty manufacturer asks Jagger's permission to market his ashes—presumably in the event of his death—in 1000

Mick gives the Stones music a certain bite.

◀

▲

*The Stones take their first
bow on the 1989 tour.
Philadelphia, Aug. 31.*

hourglasses costing $1 million apiece. Jagger
is reported to be taking the offer seriously, but is
in no apparent haste to respond.
*October, 1988. Jagger, fronting a six-piece
pickup band, mesmerizes audiences in Australia
with "an electrifying, two-and-a-half-hour
performance of 27 songs" culminating in the
Stones classic, "Gimme Shelter."
*July, 1989. Hanging from the caboose of a New
York Transit Authority subway train from
Harlem, Jagger leads the other Rolling Stones
into Grand Central Station to announce details
for assembled journalists of the 1989 twenty-fifth
anniversary tour—promoted by Canada's
Concert Productions International and Labatt
Breweries—that will earn the band in excess of
$65 million.

KEITH RICHARDS

*December 18, 1943. Keith Richard—who would
later pluralize his name, allegedly to avoid the
possibility of association with early 1960s British
pop singer Cliff Richard—is born in Dartford,
Kent, England, and later attends the same public

school as Jagger.
*1962. Richards, already steeped in the music of
American rhythm 'n' blues and electric blues
masters, drifts to London ostensibly to study art,
but actually in search of a musical education, a
mentor and a performing career. Disillusioned by
his parents' separation and divorce, and
estranged from his father—who has a reputation
as a heavy drinker and is a known associate of
the London Hell's Angels motorcycle gang—
Richards is a withdrawn, uncommunicative
young man.
    By the time he meets Jagger again, he has
already teamed up, on a nonprofessional basis,
with guitarist Brian Jones and has made inroads
into the London underground blues scene.
*1963. After their first performances, the Stones
are told to drop Jagger, because "he can't sing or
dance" and to curb Richards's anger and
surliness. He is blamed largely for the tag
attached to the band by its first critics: "They are
the voice of hooliganism."
Richards says later, "Brian (Jones) and I were the
sort of people (teachers and adults) were glad to
kick out."
*1965. Inspired largely by the success of the
Beatles, their rivals, as songwriters, Richards
insists he and Jagger take a stab
at composing their own material instead
of rehashing rare blues classics. The

guitarist takes control of the musical side, encouraging Jagger to write lyrics, and from the start of this peculiar union, with the groundbreaking rock anthem "Satisfaction," their songs catch the very spirit of this otherwise indescribable band. Jagger-Richards pieces have always had an ominous, gut-wrenching, agitated quality that makes them instantly identifiable yet almost impossible for others to perform.

*1970. Marlon, Richards's first child with Anita Pallenberg and his only son, is, at age one, a member of the Rolling Stones entourage. Says Richards, "He learned his arithmetic watching the numbers on hotel elevators, figuring how to get from the twelfth floor to the lobby to say, 'Dad needs his breakfast.'"

*1983. Richards and his father, Bert, reunite after a 20-year separation that started with the divorce of his parents when the guitarist was 18. Marlon attends school on Long Island, New York, where

he now lives with his grandfather. Richards's first daughter, Dandelion, born in 1972, lives in Britain with her mother, Anita Pallenberg.

*February, 1977. A day after entering Canada, where the band intended to record a live album at Toronto's El Mocambo, Richards is arrested in his downtown hotel room after Royal Canadian Mounted Police officers discover 22 grams of heroin in his possession. Pallenberg, his longtime common-law wife, is also charged with possession of marijuana. Richards is eventually tried on trafficking charges, but instead of being sentenced to jail or deported— which would have meant the Stones could never again play in Canada—he is ordered to perform a fund-raising concert for the Canadian National Institute for the Blind, in Oshawa, Ontario.

Federal prosecutors appeal the sentence, but are denied after the guitarist provides evidence that he is no longer addicted to drugs, and in

1979, Richards, Ron Wood and a pickup band, the New Barbarians, play two charity shows at the Oshawa Civic Centre auditorium.

*June, 1980. On the eve of the release of the *Emotional Rescue* LP, Richards, who coproduces all the band's records with Jagger, gives away some of the Stones' session secrets:

"The thing is, never allow them to feel as if they're making a Rolling Stones record. The others always think I know what I'm doing when we go into the studio, but for most of the tracks I just sit Charlie down at his drum stool and start playing. If we play for 10 or 15 minutes, the first germ has infected us. I'm like a little housefly—I go around then and infect everyone else."

*December, 1983. Richards marries New York model and actress Patti Hansen in Cabo San Lucas, Mexico. She gives birth to their first child, Theodora, in 1985. The couple's second daughter Alexandra—the guitarist's fourth child—is born in 1986.

Of marriage and children, he says, "If you're going to have kids, look after them. If you're going to dump the old lady, take care of her.

"And have as little to do with lawyers as possible."

*April, 1986. Reformed, tanned and apparently happy in his marriage, Richards admits some satisfaction in owning properties in Britain, Europe, America and Jamaica (his favorite "off-duty" hangout), a collection of cars, including a Bentley "and a couple of Ferraris" and "a lot of guitars."

He also says he enjoys jamming with Wood in pickup bands for the likes of Nona Hendryx, Tom Waits and Lonnie Mack.

*September, 1988. Richards releases *Talk Is Cheap,* his first solo album, to wide critical acclaim. Backup is provided by veteran American rock, jazz and zydeco session players, guitarists Waddy Wachtel, drummer Steve Jordan, bassist Charlie Drayton, accordionist Buckwheat Dural, singer Patti Scialfa, keyboardist Bernie Worrell and the Memphis Horns.

He blames himself for the rift with Jagger, which has fueled rumors of a Stones breakup for the past five years.

"The tension started when I cleaned up my (drug) act in '78 and '79," he says. "Mick had done an incredible job throughout the '70s shouldering the burden of the business end of the band while I was out scoring dope.

Keith and Eric Clapton trade lead singer jokes.
▼

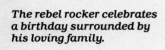

The rebel rocker celebrates a birthday surrounded by his loving family.

"But when I came back, he had gotten used to running the show and that slowly found its way under the surface (of the relationship) throughout the early 1980s."

*June, 1989. Richards is the first inductee into the "Legend" hall of fame, established by the fledgling International Rock Awards group in a concert aired live on TV across North America from New York.

CHARLIE WATTS

*June 2, 1941. Charlie Watts is born in the London suburb of Islington.
*January, 1963. Having quit the well-established London club band Blues Inc., because its busy schedule interfered with his day job in an advertising agency, Watts, a jazz and early blues devotee, is persuaded by Bill Wyman to join the Rolling Stones, just prior to their lengthy

residency at the Crawdaddy Club.
*1965. A minimalist with a unique performing style, Watts is singled out by music critics early in the Stones' career for his exceptional "feel," for being able to find the appropriate groove and propel the band without apparent effort. In the years following, as rock drum kits became larger and more elaborate, Watts amazes his followers by sticking with a basic kit—snare, a small kick drum, high hat and cymbal.

"It's all the equipment I ever use," he says. "I only ever tried to play with the band. I basically play for Mick and Keith. If I did a fill and they said, 'That's too much,' I wouldn't do it. I wasn't a part of all that theater (for which the Stones roadshow became famous). I just play the music."
*December, 1986. While other members of the Stones are involved in solo projects or collaborations with other musicians, Watts assembles a 32-piece big band comprising long-forgotten veteran British jazz musicians. He tours

with it to promote a distinctly anachronistic album, on the CBS label, of pre-be-bop jazz standards from the 1930s and '40s.

Reclusive and private, Watts has been married to the same woman, Shirley, for 25 years; they have a 21-year-old daughter, Serafina. He eschews his "invisible man" persona to indulge his pre-Stones passion for big-band music and to draw the attention of rock fans to the forms and styles on which all modern pop is based.

"Kids owe it to themselves to hear this music just once in their lives," he says.

BILL WYMAN

*October 24, 1936. Bill Wyman, the oldest Rolling Stone, is born in London.
*August, 1962. A month after the Rolling Stones' first impromptu performance in London, Wyman, then a member of a local pop group called the Cliftons, replaces Stones' founding member Dick Taylor on bass.

Another Cliftons alumnus, Tony Chapman, played a couple of shows with the Stones, but was not suited to their rough, raw style. After months of wooing, a reluctant Charlie Watts is recruited and, with Wyman, forges one of the most powerful, adaptable and enduring rhythm sections in rock 'n' roll history.
*December, 1969. Almost as quiet and retiring as Watts, and as implacable on stage, Wyman is reported to be appalled by events at the infamous Altamont concert in California and doubts that the band can continue in the face of the ensuing public outcry.

Rarely a spokesman for the Stones, nor a composer, Wyman is nonetheless believed to be its conscience, a unifying element between the often volatile Jagger and the intransigent Richards.
*June, 1975. Wyman releases his first solo album, *Monkey Grip,* to poor reviews. The followup, *Stone Alone,* in 1976, is significantly more rewarding.
*June, 1985. Devastated by the effects of multiple sclerosis on his longtime friend, composer and musician Ronnie Lane, Wyman moves directly from the Stones' *Dirty Work* sessions in Paris to promoting his pet project, *Willie and the Poor Boys,* a compendium of classic rock and rockabilly songs whose purpose is to raise funds for Action Research into Multiple Sclerosis (ARMS). The album is accompanied by a 30-minute video of several performances, featuring guest drummer and former Beatle Ringo Starr. Wyman says he'd like to extend the work into a series of albums, beginning with a revival of important soul titles from the 1960s, featuring well and lesser-known musicians.
*February, 1989. Wyman, an astute businessman and an investor in several profitable corporations, announces his intention to open a 140-seat fast-food restaurant in London.

Appropriately enough, it's to be called Sticky Fingers.
*June, 1989. Wyman, 52, marries Mandy Smith, 19, in London. Admitting he had known the beautiful blonde since she was 13, the bassist says their age difference would not prevent them from having children. Wyman divorced his first wife, Diana, in 1969, the year Smith was born. He has a 23-year-old son, Steven, from the earlier marriage.

RON WOOD

*June 1, 1947. Ron Wood is born in London.
*1969. When singer/guitarist Steve Marriott leaves psychedelic British pop band the Small Faces in 1969 to form Humble Pie, he is replaced by Rod Stewart and Ron Wood, both former members of the progressive hard-rock outfit, the Jeff Beck Group, and both a head taller than their colleagues—hence the band's name change.

Loose and rambunctious on stage, the Faces make considerable headway as arena rockers in Britain and the U.S., largely on the strength of a handful of loud and good-humored albums (*Long Player, A Nod's as Good as a Wink to a Blind Horse, Ooh La La*) in the early 1970s, and on the kudos won by Stewart, whose solo albums parallel his work with the Faces and have far greater musical merit.

Nevertheless, it is Wood's hard cracking guitar—as similar to Richards's in the Stones as Richards's is to Chuck Berry's—that propels the Faces and makes Wood a natural replacement for Mick Taylor, who quit the Stones in 1976 after two and a half albums.
*1978. On Wood's first solo LP, *I've Got My Own Album to Do,* Jagger guests on "I Can Feel the Fire," a moderate hit. Four years later, Wood's second solo effort, *Gimme Some Neck*—featuring exceptional cover portraits painted by Wood, a gifted artist—sounds more like the Faces than the Faces did themselves in their final days. His old band folds within weeks of Wood's joining the Stones as a permanent member.
*December, 1978. Wood is divorced by Chrissie, his wife of several years and mother of their two-year-old daughter, Jesse, in an uncontested adultery action naming model Jo Howard, 22.
*January, 1985. Wood marries Howard in a ribald ceremony in a village church in Buckinghamshire, England. The groom arrives wearing jeans, eating fish and chips and drinking pale ale, and promptly hands his bride her wedding present, a pair of pearl-handled Derringer pistols.

The wedding is attended by comedian Peter Cook and all the members of the Stones, except Jagger. Watts and Richards are best men. In *Rock Wives,* a kiss 'n' tell book published in 1986, Howard tells American writer Victoria Balfour that Jagger and Richards used to flirt with her before her marriage to Wood "to test her fidelity."

GOT LIVE
IF YOU WANT IT The TOUR BEGINS

Philadelphia, August 31, 1989

A line of limos snakes its way through the throngs marching on the stadium and the sound of Stones music can be heard issuing from numerous cars and boom boxes. Vendors of all sorts hustle to apply trickle-down economics, hoping to separate concert goers from any loose change they might have. Once word got out that all the Stones wives are impossibly blond, that became the look of the tour. The crowd's studded with Stone wifey blondalikes.

The show kicks off with "Start Me Up" to such a thunderous roar that most of the song is unheard. The light show kicks in, and the crowd is visibly awed as the dimensions and complexity of the stage become apparent. It's a grand construct of girders, boilers, ducts, giant-wheeled contraptions of undetermined purpose, scaffolding, catwalks and an elevator. It looks futuristic and at the same time, antiquated, turn-of-the-century.

Next up is a stiff and creaky "Bitch" and the Stones are now two-thirds of the way through the shortest set they've ever played. Jagger takes the mike for a sped-up version of "Shattered," and is almost through it when a generator goes down, taking most of his sound with it. The band promptly walks off and confusion reigns. For 11 minutes the stage remains empty and no explanation is forthcoming. Then the band returns as unceremoniously as it left. Jagger pauses to explain: "Sorry about that. We lost the power there for a bit." Then to Charlie's countdown, it's back to business with "Sad, Sad, Sad," providing room for Wood and Richards to do their chugging-guitars-in-tandem thing.

A rattle of percussion pushes "Undercover" into action; Jagger dons a guitar to help out on rhythm, and Keith and Ronnie scramble like mad covering for him. Next up is "Harlem Shuffle," featuring nifty footwork from Jagger and singer/dancers Cindy Mizelle and Lisa Fischer. This is the first time the Stones have ever done this song live—with the exception of the wake held for Ian Stewart at London's 100 Club in 1985.

"Tumbling Dice" falls out updated, a riff here, a flourish there, picks up a nicely loping groove and sets off the night's first singalong as the chant of "got to love me" rolls around the stadium and the Bics flare up in their thousands. Jagger mugs and goofs his way through "Miss You," and the reaction is one of delight in his playfulness.

A stately and commanding version of "Ruby Tuesday" comes up battling a wave of crashing guitars, to be followed by a folkish "Play with Fire," another seldom heard number that tickles the older fans. The ragged country-blues of "Dead Flowers" fuels another singalong, and Jagger allows himself a small smile of satisfaction. Despite the ongoing irritation from the erratic mix, he seems genuinely glad to be back and happy to still have it.

"One Hit to the Body" seems an odd choice for this show and doesn't really go over. It's the evening's first flat spot. "Mixed Emotions" doesn't do much to restore the heat of the moment, lurching about doggedly.

It takes the Stones' legendary flair for wide-scale spectacle to juice things up with a pair of inflatable 50-foot hookers that pop up during "Honky Tonk Women." One's blond, sits with legs crossed and a mini riding high on her thigh, cigarette in one hand and red shoe dangling seductively from her toe. The other is black or maybe Hispanic, wears teeny shorts and sparkly sneakers, sits with legs apart and humps right along to the beat.

Ron and Keith cook like microwaves on "Rock and a Hard Place," an R&B throwback that's actually off the *Steel Wheels* album; on this night, it gets over best of the new songs. "Midnight Rambler" initially sounds uncannily close to the recorded version, but it's been cut back, the long middle jam considerably shortened.

"You Can't Always Get What You Want" seems to have survived its transformation into a Levis commercial, and the crowd willingly supplies the massed voices that bolster the chorus on the record. The show again staggers with the next tune, the slow-to-the-point-of-nodding blues "Little Red Rooster." The folkish "Play with Fire" is another unexpected antique treat, Jagger giving it a vocal rife with menacing detachment.

Mick then turns over the vocal chores to Keith, and the old gunslinger seems a mite reluctant to assume the spotlight. In familiar fashion, Keith mumbles through "Gonna Walk Before They Make Me Run" and "Happy," refusing to sing on mike, constantly turning his head away, so that what comes across is a blurry vocal that fades in and out. No matter. He draws major applause mostly for just being Keith.

Swirling lights and a battery of syncopated percussion heralds "2000 Light Years from Home." It's the first time the Stones have ever played this song live. Then another first: "2000 Light Years" segues directly into "Sympathy for the Devil," a device the Stones have never used before. The stage is awash in red lights and Jagger gives us glimpses of his old, nasty self.

The mood persists through a romping version of "Paint It Black," with the keyboards double-timing and driving the thing home with a down-to-earth appeal absent from the more exotic recorded version.

Mick does a spot of navel gazing as the 1989 tour opens in Philadelphia.

▼

And then it comes. The stretch run is led off by a slightly ragged, drinking-with-the-boys version of "It's Only Rock 'n' Roll," then the heat turns up another notch for "Brown Sugar," another singalong, or chantalong in this case, with the song's "yeah, yeah, yeah, woo" chorus. Everybody's standing, and even between songs, you can't hear much through the excited noise. All night the momentum has built nicely, despite the glitches, and now there's no doubt in anyone's mind that they are part of an EVENT.

As Keith and Ron unlimber the familiar chords to "Satisfaction," the noise level again rises to the point where the band can barely be heard. There's a moment of relative hush, then with a loud whoosh, rockets burst from the twin towers to explode in gaily colored balls of light as the Rolling Stones whale into "Jumping Jack Flash"

with everything they have left. Which is considerable, Jagger dragging out the final moments with spirited fancy dancing. Then just like that, it's over. They're gone. In a flash.

Toronto, September 3 & 4, 1989

The Toronto dates are at Exhibition Stadium, and attract more than 60,000 fans each night. The crowd is much like that in Philadelphia, a mix of age and beauty. Hundreds of bicycles are chained to the wrought-iron fencing of the Dufferin Gates; a white vintage Rolls, threading its way through the mob, narrowly misses creaming a number of them. The occupants are raffish-looking thirty-somethings, the thickness of their stock portfolios away from the street-fighting men they used to be.

Sunday night the Stones bound onstage to a sea of waving arms and a roar of screaming voices, wearing much the same getup as in Philly. What's very different and apparent from the opening chords is the superiority of the sound mix here. There isn't even the barest hint of the muzzies as the band tears into "Bitch," which comes over a lot looser, especially on Monday night. Out of respect for its equipment-destroying properties, "Shattered" is dropped from Sunday's set and its place taken by "Gimme Shelter," inserted further down the set list. "Sad, Sad, Sad" opens with the raunchy blues chording that typifies the Stones' seventies sound. At one point, Keith smiles at the crowd and the place goes crazy.

On both nights in Toronto, Ron Wood plays most of the leads while Keith is content to lay back and add the ornamentation. The set rolls briskly on through "Undercover," after which Jagger takes time out for a cheeky reference to his wicked past. "I was a little bit worried," he confides, "when I saw Mrs. Mulroney backstage, but everything's cool." Mrs. Mulroney is Mila, the wife of the current Canadian prime minister and nothing at all like Margaret Trudeau, the wife of a previous prime minister, with whom Jagger is alleged to have dallied when the Stones last visited Canada in 1977.

The Rolling Stones' first concert in Canada in a decade continues to build its momentum, unimpeded by sound problems. "Harlem Shuffle," "Tumbling Dice," and "Miss You" roll by with power and precision. Jagger, whirling and punching air in his green leather greatcoat, remains an intense, balletic and magnetic presence, arousing mystery and hormones with his angular arm gestures and suggestive dalliances at stage front. His voice is still capable of lewd possibilities and jacks up songs like "Midnight Rambler" and "Brown Sugar" into the sexual stratosphere.

"Ruby Tuesday" provides the most elegant moment, carried aloft on Mick's wistful croon and the understated playing of the group. Then it was back to menace and sardonic inflections with "Play with Fire," "Dead Flowers" and "One Hit to the Body." With the help of Keith's and Ron's patented power chording and Bill's and Charlie's rock-steady rhythm foundation, Jagger convinces the crowd that when it comes to rock 'n' roll legitimacy, attitude still has it all over youth.

Attitude and improved sound gets "One Hit to the Body" across in impressive style, while the self-evident charms of "Honky Tonk Women" survives sloppy playing by Wood and the refusal of one of the monster hookers to dance. "Midnight Rambler" is again presented in abbreviated fashion and will likely stay that way for the duration. "Rock and a Hard Place" is handled with assurance and fits easily into the motif. "You Can't Always Get What You Want" is rendered in a stately and dramatic fashion, Jagger taking a few moments to conduct the crowd chorus.

While the Stones records have been frustratingly inconsistent, the group's reputation as a live act has been outstanding, and the Toronto shows only confirm that. Jagger again gives "Play with Fire" a deliberately, scary-sounding treatment, then abruptly changes the mood by grabbing the mike and saying, "What can I tell you? I've got to go and change me knickers." Then it's Keith's turn again to mumble and mangle his way through "Gotta Walk Before They Make Me Run" and "Happy."

The Stones tribute to sixties psychedelia—"2000 Light Years from Home"—arrives in swirling, pulsating lights of an intensity and color only dreamed of in that decade. It's a visual more than a musical crowd pleaser, and its place on the set list isn't solid.

Jagger prances through "Sympathy for the Devil," devilish as can be, then pumps up the pace as he races through "Paint It Black." He gears down a notch so the singalong can keep up on the chorus for "Gimme Shelter," then grabs that singalong and carries it over into "It's Only Rock 'n' Roll."

From here on in, every song is an occasion for the crowd to join in, and they're from far enough back in the Stones catalogue that everyone knows the words. Then it's good night and thank you, and as the Stones leave the stage, the crowd noise gets really LOUD. Thankfully only for mere minutes. Jagger and the boys quickly return to storm through an extended take of "Jumping Jack Flash."

METAMORPHOSIS
The Once and Future Stones

The Rolling Stones came from a time when rock music spurred on and helped shape an entire culture. It was central to the changes of society in a way nothing, and certainly no form of music, has been since. Rock has always been the music of turbulence, and for a short time back there, history caught the beat.

Ironically the Stones typify the state of rock as it heads into the nineties. Rock has turned around and broken most of its own cardinal rules, yet it still survives on its bedrock guts and will to thrill. It's not afraid to believe in itself. Rock may have become big business but it still has no fixed address, no set agenda. It has lots of names, labels; it has lots of history, some of it proud.

But it still can't be tied down, classified with any surety. It's still our cultural orphan at the far end of respectability. It has history but no home. It lives in exile on main street.

GREG QUILL is an entertainment writer and music critic for the *Toronto Star*. During the 1970s he was a songwriter/guitarist fronting bands in Canada and his native Australia, where he recorded several albums and had a number of chart successes. Many of his songs have been recorded by other Australian artists, as well as American and British performers.

Quill holds a BA in English Language and Literature from the University of Sydney, and was the first rock songwriter in his country to be awarded a travel/study grant by the Australian Council for the Arts.

He has written feature articles, reviews and opinion pieces for several Canadian magazines since settling in Toronto in 1976, and he edited the Canadian rock publications *Music Express* (now *Rock Express*) and *Graffiti* in the early 1980s.

Quill quit performing and recording in 1982. His most recent book for Kamin & Howell Inc. was on Michael Jackson in 1988.

LENNY STOUTE is a Toronto-based freelance entertainment writer who's interviewed most of the major acts of the last 15 years. He has edited *Music Express, Hot Sounds* and *Metallion* magazines, and currently contributes to a wide array of Canadian and U.S. newspapers and magazines, including the *Toronto Star* and New York's *Metal Hammer*.

Stoute is currently assembling a book of short stories, many of which are set in the world of rock'n'roll.

KAMIN & HOWELL INC.
is one of the world's leading packagers
and publishers of books.
They have produced more than 70 titles.